12 Power Principles for Administrative Professionals

Dr. Amanda Goodson

AMANDA GOODSON
Goodson Leadership Mini-books ™

ISBN-13: 978-0615795690
ISBN-10: 0615795692

Printed in the U.S.A.

Third Edition

12 Power Principles for Administrative Professionals

Dr. Amanda Goodson

AMANDA GOODSON
Goodson Leadership Mini-books ™

Table of Contents

Acknowledgements

I dedicate this book to Regina Grant and Dena Yell for their tireless efforts in support of executive leaders. Their work and research served as a platform from which to write this book. Words cannot express the thanks for how they were so selfless toward being a supporter toward major efforts in the aerospace arena for our country. I especially thank them and all the wonderful people who supported or partnered with me personally during my time at NASA.

Administrative professionals in Tucson – you know who you are (thank you for inspiring me to write this book)!

To all leaders, thank you for your willingness and patience with your administrative professional.

And to my family and friends– thank you, as well.

Dr. Amanda Goodson

Introduction

Want to be the best administrative professional around? Want principles to unlock your full potential and influence others in a more powerful way? Want a compelling career where you are needed, noticed, and great? You should know that you are a person of significance and have great potential. This book is developed to give you principles to help you soar and do great things. Whether you want to be a better professional, parent, student or employee – this book will help you navigate through the ridges to a place of confidence and contentment.

I believe that you already have exactly what you need inside of you to be the best you. You just need a little boost, tweaking, education or your confidence built to see the greatness that lies within. Sometimes all that's needed is just a few adjustments and some enlightenment to see it.

The principles in this book are written in a clear concise format to make you think and give you what you need to move from where you are to a better place in your career and life. Please maintain an open mind as you read these pages, and implement what you learn immediately to start the process of becoming a better you.

This book contains several keys to assist you in growing to your full potential. Administrative professionals who use this book will see remarkable improvement in their situations, relationships and their performance at many levels. Those who act on what they learn will develop the skills needed to reach peak states within the organizations they serve.

I believe we have all been granted the ability to accomplish great things. Greatness has many facets and levels. Greatness carries power; and the power to carry out our tasks can be done well with the right desire.

The information in this mini book, *12 Power Principles for Office (Administrative) Professionals*, will serve to equip you with tools that will provide valuable insights into how to support your organization or family with greatness. Administrative professionals who use these principles will have an opportunity to transform themselves and others around them on a routine basis. Administrative professionals who have a great attitude, create the right atmosphere, use their unlimited potential, use their roadmap, know when to innovate and influence others, think critically, make a difference in excellence, and are honest champions.

This book is meant to arouse your thinking and cause you to be more creative, enhance your knowledge base, and develop a style that will impact others around you with power. As you read these pages, keep an open mind so that you will be able to see how the principles highlighted will transform you, assist you in learning new skills to enhance your thinking, and will place you in a position to touch those whose lives you influence. I have provided you with relevant stories that will help your journey, and I have added information for emphasis.

At the end of each chapter, I have provided space for your personal reflections and notes. Enjoy reading and learning how to reach your place of greatness!!

1. Attitude for Success

I would like to introduce you to Mrs. H. She is one of the most influential and powerful people around in her workplace and community. She is known as Mrs. Encourager. She is a strong encourager, motivator, and inspires others around her in a powerful way on a routine basis. I have added some things to the story in order to better emphasize this principle.

One day, she was asked to speak to a group of people about how she got such a great attitude. She was a little reserved about it because she had never spoken in front of a crowd like that before. After a few days of thinking about it, she decided to do it.

When the day came for her to speak before the crowd, she stood there and asked them the following sequence of questions:

- What do you want out of life?
- Who do you want to impact in profound ways over the next few years?
- What are your dreams and desires?
- How many of you have had them come to pass exactly like you expected?

After asking for a show of hands after each question, she then asked:

- How many of you are still dreaming and expect for your dreams to come true in the near future?

The audience responded with an affirmation of a hearty applause.

She continued to talk about her dreams. With excitement, she began to tell her story. "There was a time that I wanted to be a singer and stand in front of the crowds and bring joy to them. I wanted raving fans who would just love to hear me sing and have good clean fun.

I loved to sing anything from opera, to jazz to pop songs. I was pretty good at it, but never got my Broadway debut. I would stand in front of the mirror and practice over and over again. I would practice my best moves and my facial expressions. I would lean my body back really far to reach the high notes and bend down or to the side for the low notes.

I would anticipate the crowds' response to my singing and would take appropriate pauses for applause. I would sing in the shower, down the street, in the malls. It was a lot of fun to get the practice, but the dream never fully came to pass the way I thought it would.

One day, I went to a class about having a great self-image and self-projection. The teacher was so fascinating that I decided that I wanted to be a public speaker instead of a singer. I loved hearing others speak. It seemed right for me.

Not only did I want to speak nationally, I also wanted to be a speaker for the masses and travel around the world. I would write my speeches on 3x5 cards and would practice what I wrote about when visiting uncommon places. When I was in the car at a red light, I would pull out my cards and rehearse. I would keep them in my purse and when I was on a break from work, I would go through them. I would find myself, in the mornings, reading them and just before bed, reading them.

I even memorized the speeches on the cards and practiced my speeches over and over again. I would record them on CDs, and if I made a mistake, I would make myself re-record the speech over until it was perfect. I would take classes on my own to help me get better. If there was a difficult word or phrase that sounded weird, I would change it up to a better word or phrase. Laughter is important to me, so I would add humorous stories or lines every chance I got when I wrote my speeches.

I envisioned myself in front of many people. My speeches would change many lives – I thought – so I had to be the best. I wanted to inspire others into action and cause their lives to catapult into someone they never thought they would be. I thought they would love to hear what I had to say because it would not only make them feel great, but it would make them greater too!

I even went to a local studio once and made a CD series of my favorite speeches. The gentleman at the studio was a singer too, and he helped me to make a jingle to put as part of the intro to my CD series. I wrote on topics called Zero Gravity, Parachute Packer and Above the Storm, among many others. I was a dreamer. I loved it!!

The more I dreamed, the farther it seemed that my dream would not come into reality as quickly as I had expected. The more I thought about it, the more I thought that my dream was in the distant future. (But I never gave up.)

After a few years, I got married, had a child and my priorities shifted. I moved to a new job assignment, which also shifted my priorities.

With all of that happening, I had to make a decision. I decided to be silent and not give my best in my assignments. I was in silent rebellion because I wanted my dreams to come true – right now. I told myself that I should have it all. I thought I needed to reserve my best for my dreams and my future; not in my current situation. After all, I am a pretty nice person and had a clear vision for my future – I should reserve my best for later.

Life's challenges continued to happen. The dream had not come like I thought it should. I had to make a decision and make it fast. I was at a fork in the road. On the one path, I could continue to have this attitude of being laid back; or I would choose the other path and I could shift and be the best me ever; right now.

I could use my skills right where I was and see my audience differently. I decided to make a massive change in my life, and I decided to be great right now; right where I am. I decided to be a great employee, mother and wife. I decided to be a great speaker in the community. I decided to transform my thinking for the better.

I gave myself the best gift ever. I sought to have the right attitude. Having a great attitude is everything. With the right attitude, you can achieve almost anything."

With tears in her eyes, she said: "Having the right attitude caused me to be envied, prosperous and get favor on my job. The right attitude allowed me to see myself as great; no matter what happened around me. My attitude allowed me to build a newfound happiness and a compelling future."

She pointed out that she has her dream, and it is packaged in a great way. She is a great speaker – all that hard work paid off. She further stated that she is allowed to speak for groups in the community on a weekly basis. She loves it, and they enjoy her!!

Finally, she asked, "What about you? Which path have you chosen? Will you enjoy the process and reach the greatest destiny ever? The choice is yours – that is one thing that no one can take away from you – the ability to make a choice. So….choose."

Below are my recommended attitudes that will cause you to soar and be better in every area of your life. In the reflections section, please feel free to add to this list. Read this list often and enjoy your shift:

- Be a significant participant in the greater good – no complaining please.
- Be a winner by being kind, loving and laughing – it may be contagious.
- Be a learner – everything you hear or see will be a teacher for you. You can put your learning into three buckets:

1. Apply it now
2. Improve the idea and apply it later
3. Never do it that way

- Learn from your mistakes, learn from others, and learn from appropriate media
- Be courteous to everyone – you never know who will be your boss, teammate or community leader one day.
- Be steady – it brings stability to an organization.
- Be creative – appropriate creativity and innovation will cause an organization to excel and exceed in awesome ways.
- Be flexible – everything will not always go your way. If necessary, be willing to change in order to make the organization do well in meeting challenges and goals.
- Be efficient – do your best, be your best and think your best.
- Be faithful – never give up on doing the right thing.
- Be loyal – never stop supporting your leader when they need it. (If they are unethical or rude, you may need to take appropriate action.)
- Be meek – meekness is humility under control. Stay controlled in your demeanor and actions.
- Be strong – be a person of courage in every situation. If you need help, ask for it from the right mentor or coach. As you are

faithful, your trials and struggles will work endurance and patience in you.

- Be confident – it will breed excellence in you.
- Be selfless – on many occasions, it will not be about you. Be willing to do what it takes to get the job done. Also, try to see things from another person's perspective.
- Be giving – give and it will be given back to you in some way. Giving is best served with a great attitude.
- Have passion – it will fuel you.
- Have fun – laugh a lot. People will see energy in your laughter and want you around.

Administrative Reflections:

What additional things will you do to have a better attitude? What would you add to the list in this chapter as a characteristic of a great attitude? List at least 5.

2. Transform Yourself

I was in a place of personal and professional transformation and a significant move. My son was about five years old at the time. He loved some things around him which he held dearly and had a fondness of other things in his surroundings /environment. Butterflies were on neither list. (Chuckle)

During one of the many times when we were moving, he would stop me and ask the question, in his manner of speaking: "Mommie – why do cammerpillers turn into butterplys? Why mommie?!"

I looked at him with a smile, then I put down the bag I was packing to answer his question. As I looked at him, I could see that his dark brown eyes seemed to be amazed with caterpillars, although he did not like them. I paused, smiled while I took a seat next to him in our family room and simply answered, "It's because they are destined to soar. Yep, they are destined to soar!"

Later in school, he learned about the process that the caterpillar goes through to transform into such a beautiful creature. This lesson helped him learn about the process it takes to reach his destiny.

You know the story: the butterfly once started out as a little worm, crawling on the ground everywhere it went. It had to look up to other things around it – a lot. It might have even seen a butterfly; but didn't know that it would eventually become the very same being that soared above it. The caterpillar could slowly and graciously crawl up and down trees, lay on leaves and on sidewalks.

Then in the next part of the process, it finds a home on a tree branch, or some place similar, and becomes covered by a web called a cocoon. This is its home for a time -- until it is time to emerge. The cocoon is a place of growth and waiting. The cocoon protects and provides a place of safety from harmful elements.

As the grand day approaches for the butterfly to emerge from its cocoon, it has to continue to go through a process of coming out slowly. I understand that if the butterfly comes out too soon and is not fully developed yet, coming out too soon will cause the destiny of the butterfly to be shortened. If the butterfly stays in the cocoon too long, its destiny will never emerge and its life will end.

Finally, the beautiful butterfly will emerge with regal brilliance and vitality. With bright vibrant colors of yellow, orange, blue, black, and green, it soars above the crowd, never taking pause about the process of becoming or never trying to become a caterpillar again. In fact, it is impossible to go back. The butterfly has reached its potential and emerged in excellence and greatness. It is destined to soar.

This process speaks so much about our lives and the process we go through as we move into different assignments, have a family or support the community. Doesn't it?

Many of us are in a stage of development and transformation just like the butterfly. We might be just starting out in our careers or in a new effort at work, home or in our community. If we are just starting, our vision will not be a reality just yet – hold on; it is coming. Our experiences may seem at a distance - but great is coming; the ability to soar is coming. We may be lying along the road or in a tree dreaming about what might come. And that is good thing to do. Keep dreaming - do not stop!

You might be in a cocoon stage in your life or career. It might seem like you are going nowhere fast or that you are stagnant. Keep holding on. You might be growing in an environment suited to protect you from the dangers that the growth process demands. You may be in a learning pattern just waiting to come out one day. You might just be in the phase where tough times require you to be patient and wait. Nonetheless, your time is surely coming to peek your wings through the web of life and soar.

You may even be in the butterfly stage where you are soaring above the rest with your beautifully colored wings and with a sway that others notice. Enjoy that process.

Again notice what phase you are in by noticing your surroundings – you will see clues. Whether you are there already or for those on the way to being a butterfly, please notice where you are and make the best of it right now. Your day to soar is coming quickly.

No matter your stage or station in life, you must transform yourself in a place of greatness and be prepared to step up the challenges that each stage demands.

Here is what Odetta Scott, co-author of *How to Unlock Your Full Potential*, says about butterfly transformation:

"I believe we have the ability to do everything to meet our destined purpose in life. We have the ability to do mighty things in our work, home, and community when we put forth the effort. We may go through difficult times, but we should not give up on being our best.

Our inherent capability is just like the story of the transformation process from a caterpillar to a butterfly. I believe we have superior, powerful, and effective ability mapped right inside of us. As we seek our destiny, I believe that we discover our full purpose. As we become like the butterfly, we can soar higher and make things happen around us that we never thought we could.

The caterpillar has such a different perspective on life. It has a limited view and limited self-expectation. The caterpillar cannot think in extremes because its expectations are low, slow, and lacking. Although the caterpillar is needed, the inherent sense and the nature of the caterpillar is one of passive mediocrity. In fact, not much happens at the caterpillar level.

Later, in the cocoon stage, it may seem as if movement has ceased and the growth has been severely hindered. This is a stage of uncertainty and uneasiness. This stage might seem to hinder your ability to grow and use your gifts as you need to. One may feel constricted and limited in their growth potential.

At the butterfly stage, one emerges to a place of beauty and excellence. The ability of the butterfly is no longer hindered but released to pollinate and affect others around it. The butterfly has a different perspective in life. Its perspective is one of higher expectations, security, ease in flight, and excelling.

The butterfly emerges to occupy a space that shows great promise, destiny, and awe. It has been released from its cocoon and is now unlocked and able to reach its full potential by getting up, having a different perspective on life, and taking on the opportunity to soar in life!

I want to take a pause here to say this–for those who think they cannot be good at doing something, this is for you. Know ahead of time what you are awesome and capable of power, creative potential, and excellent ability. When your thoughts are focused on the right destination, you will achieve greatness!"

So, see yourself as being transformed already. If you are not there yet, it will be coming soon. Transformation takes place in your mind first. If you see yourself as transformed, then act that way. Get ready; set; now, transform!!

Administrative Reflections:

In the space below, list 3 to 5 additional thoughts about transforming your life right now and achieving great results. What are your expectations for the future? In what areas are you becoming a butterfly? (List 3-5)

3. Create the Right Atmosphere

Do you think of yourself as an atmosphere changer? What does atmosphere mean to you? I like to think of atmosphere as the space or climate around you that you have the ability to influence and affect. The atmosphere is the invisible circle around you that will cause others to respond to the climate you create in your circle. For instance, if you are joyous, the atmosphere around you will be joyous – unhappiness cannot enter. If you are peaceful, then peace will permeate your atmosphere – anger cannot live long. When you create a harmonious environment, then chaos has to go away.

I used to play in a band. I played the clarinet and the piano. When we played, we created an environment or climate for the listeners around us. When I was in the marching band, we would practice on the school lawns and at times on the football field. We would lift our feet and legs to a cadence conducted by the band director. "One, two, three, four; turn", I would hear as the conductor counted off a cadence for us to march. When it was time for us to play our instruments, then we would play a tune familiar to the football fans.

At the games, the football players would create an atmosphere of competition and adventure. When they were winning, the crowds would be more excited than ever. The atmosphere was set for us at half time. During half time, we would get on the field and play. The fans would clap to the music and some would sing to our songs. We would do fancy moves, special turns and unique routines to get the crowd more excited.

I recall a time that I had to do a special move that I call the pivot and turn. I was to march forward for eight counts, then on the ball of my foot, turn quickly to the left and position myself to make a predetermined letter or symbol for our school. The fake grass was slippery, and you can imagine what happened.

Our band was really good we were successful at creating an atmosphere of fun and excitement at the games.

The cheerleaders would pump up the crowds and get us all up on our feet. They would yell, "Give me a V; give me an I; give me a C; give me a T; give me an O; give me a R; give me a Y. What does it spell? VICTORY! What do you have? VICTORY! What does it spell? VICTORY!! YEAH!!" We would scream at the top of our lungs, clap our hands, laugh, give our neighbors a high five, and then move from side to side dancing to the rhythm.

That is atmosphere. The football team created the atmosphere of winning, the band created the atmosphere of excitement, and the cheerleaders created the atmosphere of victory.

You can do it all. You are a player of sorts – you are on a winning team if you choose to think that way. You are an exciting musician playing an instrument to create harmony in your organization, and of course, you cheer others (including your bosses) on to success!!

Creating the right atmosphere includes:

- A willingness to be happy when others are not.

- Coming to work with a positive attitude charged for the day and ready to make a difference.

- The ability to stay on track and create harmony when others are marching to the wrong tune.

- A willingness to be peaceful and steady in uncertain times.

- Understanding that change is inevitable, and the way you see it will affect others.

- Being congenial, poised and profession at all times.

- Leading through your positive support to others and to your boss.

You are definitely an atmosphere changer! Be someone others want to be around. Now, go. Create an atmosphere shift around you today!!

Administrative Reflections:

In the space below, list 3 to 5 additional thoughts about creating the right atmosphere and how this characteristic enhances your excellence as an administrative professional. In what areas can you make improvements? (List 3-5)

4. Unlimited Potential

I have a question for you. Where does your potential stop? Can you see yourself with unlimited potential? I do.

So many people do not see the potential that exists within. The mind is an awesome engine that can be used to achieve many great things. Limits are defined by what we create in our minds. You have heard the old adage – if you think you can't, then you are right. The opposite is true as well – if you think you can – then you are right!

So, what do you think about your self? Do you see yourself reaching greatness and high heights? If so, you are well on the way. If not, then no problem.

When you finish reading this paragraph, I would like for you to close your eyes and start dreaming about what might be. I would like you to go to a special place like an island. Would you like to scuba dive or drive a plane? What about a space ship? Would you like to fly in one of those? Maybe you are the more gentle type, and you would like to be a better gardner or an expert at something.

In any case, you can have almost anything you want if you can see it in your mind. Nearly all of the world's greatest discoveries started as a thought. Imagine a world with the modern conveniences that would not have been invented or discovered without exercising the full potential within.

Use your mind to visualize a great future for yourself. Write down your dream. Where do you expect to be in three years? Five? Ten? Fifty, if you dare?

Whatever you focus your mind upon is what you will experience. If you see yourself as not moving forward in life, then you will experience just that. If you see yourself experiencing great things in life, then you will experience that also!

If you could have/do/be anything you want, what would that be? Write it down. Flow freely and continue to pursue it like you are purposed to do it and from that dream you will experience a great journey and your destiny will emerge.

Leader Reflections:

Write down your vision statement and what you believe your purpose is. Your vision statement should be a clear concise statement that causes you to start with an end in mind like this:

"My vision is to:

_____
_____
_____
_____

and enjoy the journey"

5. Have a Roadmap

Now that you have a documented vision, in order for you to achieve that vision with more precision, you should have a roadmap. Remember, while pursuing the vision, you will experience potholes, detours and some hiccups; they come as strengthening exercises for you.

Let's take a road trip. My vision is for us to drive to sunny Orlando, Florida. We currently live in Las Angeles, California and because we have time, we choose to drive to Florida. Here are the supplies we may need:

- Reliable transportation
- Map or GPS
- Clothes/shoes/personal items
- Money for gas, food and incidentals

- Place to spend the night for breaks
- Water
- Fix-a-flat (and other things for our ride)
- Health and safety items
- Entertainment items

Okay, we have nearly all we need to go on our trip. So, let's get started. It's during the spring season of the year, and as we are driving along, we notice that the weather is pretty nice. The sky is bright, sunny and the weather is about 82 degrees in the daytime and about 63 degrees at night; perfect for travelling. We have chosen to stop in Arizona to see the Grand Canyon; Houston, Texas; and then New Orleans, Louisiana along the way.

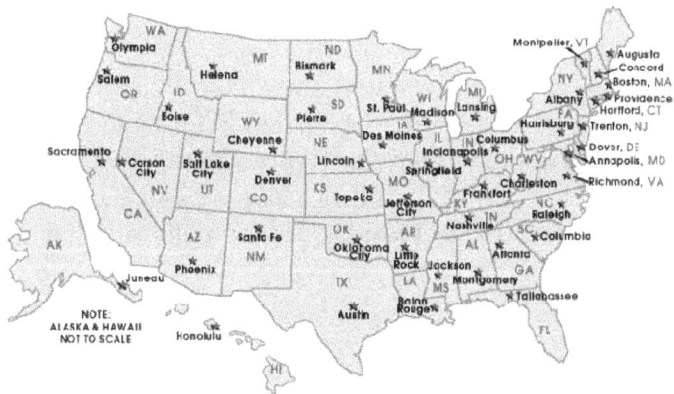

Note: Map taken from Google Images -
www.50states.com

We have gone on-line and chosen hotels right off the highway route for us to spend the night during our travels. We also have selected several places to eat during our stops and have selected tours of each city that we plan to visit.

Everything is going just as we planned. We left Los Angeles on time and arrived in Arizona at the Grand Canyon just as planned. We decided to stop for a couple of days in Arizona and took a guided tour of the canyon. We also took a VIP helicopter ride of the west rim. We were so in awe of the trip that we decided to stay an extra day.

Now, it's time to move on toward Houston, Texas. We wanted to tour the NASA Johnson Space Center to see a real space vehicle and possibly get some autographs of astronauts. On our way to Houston, Texas, the weather was favorable. It was 78 degrees during the day and 60 degrees at night. We could deal with that!

Finally, we see the welcome sign that says, "Welcome to Texas!" We are happy and looking forward to our next stop.

Suddenly, the highway signs read, Dallas 10 miles away. Oops! We were going to Houston; NOT Dallas. Something must have happened. We did not envision ourselves going to Dallas. We wanted to go to Houston. "Maybe we should have flown," says one of our travelling friends.

Okay; it is now time for a course correction. Without realizing it, the GPS had been reprogrammed. We needed a course correction right away. After all, we had a tour planned and it was already pre-paid. Our tour was to start on the next morning, but we were certain we could make it!

Although we had to take extra time on our trip because of our detour, we could still get to our interim destination on schedule as planned. Also, we got a chance to see some lovely scenery and learn more about Texas along the way.

Whew, that was close! We needed to check our GPS and make sure it was calibrated and programmed properly. Okay, it is. Let's proceed.

We finally arrived in New Orleans, and later we arrived in Orlando without a hitch. Mickey Mouse and Minnie Mouse were in tact. The detours and bumps along our path didn't affect us much. The resort that we saw in the photos did not totally look the way we envisioned. Many parts were better, others were similar to our photos and others were worn. In the final analysis, it was a great place!! We thoroughly enjoyed our stay. We had our own personal tour guide. He was wonderful. He was very kind, up close and personal, and very helpful.

He gave us the assurance that our stay would be great and that he would help us navigate through anything we might encounter.

Life works like that. You will have a clear vision and purpose, but there will be some detours along the way. Do not let your challenges derail your plan. Eventually, you will arrive at an awesome destination. It may look different than you originally pictured, but all in all, it will be great for you. For us, the best part was the journey.

Administrative Reflections:

In the space below, develop a road map that will assist you in reaching your vision (see the previous chapter). Choose 3-5 clearly defined/documented goals (stopping places) along the way that would be meaningful to your personal or professional growth.

6. Know When to Innovate

In today's times, innovation is critical to moving an organization to the next level. Innovation is the ability to take a common idea and produce uncommon results; the ability to make things once thought to be impossible, possible; or the ability to influence a market or business in ways that excel expectations in remarkable ways.

Innovation is needed all around us. Innovations have produced our media network, revolutionized the car industry, and have created clean energy for us to continue to thrive in our world.

You are innovative as well. When was the last time you saw something that needed to be repaired or that needed a better solution, and you just took care of it yourself? What about all of those "as seen on TV"

items we see on the television? What is that about?
Innovation!

Now, some of the items I see on TV are nice, but I
have no use for them. I would not be interested in
purchasing them - even if I buy one and get one free
with shipping and handling paid.

Yes, there are some items that cause me to take
pause and definitely would be useful for me if I had
it yesterday. Others, I would use over and over
again if I had them at my disposal.

Innovations are like that. Some are not useful in the
market space where we are; others are a day too late;
and still others are just right.

It is up to us to find the right innovative thought and
apply it at the right time in the right way. You have
greatness within you, and you can do it.

You should make a list of things around you that
need to get better on the left side of your page. At
the top, make columns (yes; you may make an Excel
spread sheet for this one), with the labels:

- Do nothing about this.

- Too late for this one, wait for another
  opportunity.

- Share this idea with someone else who will
  be able to use it.

- Act NOW!

Notice the things that need to be acted on right away and act now! People are waiting on your innovation to make their jobs or activities better.

Innovations include great ideas about how to fix a problem, great suggestions on how to move forward, new thoughts about a new objective that will save large amounts of resources, or even a renewed approach to a current activity.

When you have an innovation, others might not appreciate your creativity just yet. Wait or tell someone else, and your innovative idea will flourish!

Now, have fun and go innovate!!

Administrative Reflections:

In the space below, list additional reflections on your thoughts about innovation. Recall a recent situation where you think you could have a better idea to solve a challenge and make a recommended list with your solutions. (List 3-5)

7. Influence Others

Who is the one person or persons who influenced you the most? Influence can be defined as something that can change a person's thinking, course of activity, or cause them to seek new ways of doing things. With your influence and willingness to create the right atmosphere around you, things could be so much better where you are.

Being a person of influence carries power and weight. People of influence are known as "people to get to know". In order to be a person of influence, you should have the following qualities:

- Know your craft.

- Have a positive attitude.

- Be a good communicator (connect with people).

- Conduct yourself so that others will notice (professional presence).

- Have people skills – understand that each person is different – and treat them accordingly.

- Rise above the little things and the bigger ones too (quote by: Joan Muhammad).

- Make everything you do work well for the good of the organization and others.

- Value your boss, customers, peers and co-workers.

- Be willing.

- Seek excellence in all you do; then, re-evaluate and make corrections whenever necessary.

- Navigate the ridges well.

- Treat everyone with dignity and respect.

- Be a mentor or coach for them.

- Be willing to grow, live, and learn.

- Be ethical.

- Smile genuinely.

There have been several administrative professionals who have influenced me. Once, I was traveling and needed to change my plans. It turned out that my plans needed to be changed several times. I would call the office and ask for my travel plans to be changed, and then an hour later my plans needed to be changed again. Then after a couple of days, I needed them to change again.

I know it might be frustrating to have so many changes with the numbers of people that some have to support, but a kind, balanced response will go a long way.

My administrative assistant just said, "Okay; I will take care of it. No problem." Little did she know that I had a sickness in my family and needed to change quickly to see the sick family member.

My trip went as planned. All was well, and after a few months, my family member got well and continues to do well. I needed to be there for my mother, and an administrative professional helped make that happen without any complaints. Thank you for that! I was influenced to treat people well (especially people of power); no matter what; because my kindness will influence them to be kind to me in return, and to others also.

Administrative Reflections:

In the space below, list additional reflections on your thoughts about influencing others. Recall a time when you influenced others and make a list. Make a list of 3 to 5 other people who have influenced you.

8. Think Critically (Confidently)

Administrative professionals may recognize that they are also powerful ambassadors with the innate ability to think critically with the highest level of confidence. Critical thinking usually requires one look at several angles of an opportunity, develop top possible alternatives (keep in mind risk, resources and objectives), and to provide a compelling solution for all to enjoy and implement.

Additionally, confident critical thinkers should boldly make recommendations for improvements and recommend changes that will compel others to think differently, as well as move the organization in a way that causes leadership to navigate tough territory with ease. When I consider critical thinking, I am reminded of the role of an ambassador.

As I reflect on ambassadorship, an ambassador is typically an individual who has been sent as a high official, a delegate, a messenger, or an emissary to a particular place with an assignment from the government or organization that they support. The ambassador is vital to the success of an organization or government. Sometimes, ambassadors are assigned to be an instrument of peace, and at other times they carry an important message abroad to other governments. In some cultures, only those who would be willing to give careful consideration to the risk of their lives and invest all would be considered worthy of such an assignment.

A true ambassador is one who will be willing to represent their government, country, or organization with their best efforts in order to carry out the assigned mission or message in an outstanding way. This isn't just the act of giving up all their material wealth and possessions, but total and absolute unconditional surrender of self to complete their assignment.

An ambassador's commitment has to be without any reservations. In order to be a true ambassador of power, a person must be willing to lead or advocate for an assigned cause for the government or the organization that they represent in a way that gets results.

An ambassador is often assigned to go into areas that are considered to be harsh and dangerous in order to be an influence for their government or organization. At other times, the assignment may seem easy. In either case, the ambassador understands that he or she has been charged with an assignment to complete and successfully influence the territory around them.

With this understanding, and with proper training, clear vision, and the goals of the organization, the ambassador is fully equipped as they are going through their delegated assignment. They have the assurance of outstanding success. Critical thinking is needed in completing assignments with confidence. One should look at the assignment, break it down into smaller parts, and apply unique innovative approaches in creating an excellent opportunity for success in the business arena, home or community

In being better in your assignments, see yourself as an ambassador of power on an important assignment or task for your organization and influence using the ambassador mindset. Take your assignment seriously, transform the way you think about the assignment, and focus on being outstanding.

Remember that you should lead with the mindset of an ambassador. Be able to think critically and with the type of sway that conveys your ability to your country, business, and community.

Administrative Reflections:

In the space below, list the assignment you have that will put you in a position to serve your organization with integrity as a critical thinker and with the confidence of an ambassador?

9. Be Different and Excellent

I know many people who are determined to be different. They dress differently than others, they wear different hairstyles, and they seek to distinguish themselves from the pack by doing ordinary things in a more extraordinary way.

Some are so different that they shine above the rest. It is good to be different and put a spin on things as an administrative professional. However, be careful not to be different in areas where only common approaches are wanted. You definitely want to be distinguished, but not inappropriately.

Being different and excellent at the same time suggests the following:

- Be well prepared, organized and keep others on track.

- Know whom you are supporting and what your customer/boss/leader needs.

- Know the personality and style of the customer/leader and seek to compliment it with your style.

- Be willing to shift, change and hang in there during difficulties.

- Seize opportunities to learn something new.

- Do what you do above the rest (without gloating).

- Be conscientious.

- Challenge yourself to improve constantly.

- Seek answers and solutions to pressing needs. Make a difference.

- Use your uniqueness to benefit the organization at the proper times and in proper ways.

- Be willing to deal with difficult people with grace and a calm attitude.

- Navigate the ridges with ease and a smile.

- Be flexible with customers/leaders, convey a will-do and a can-do attitude.

Frederick Cross, co-author of *How to Unlock your Full Potential – Eleven Keys to Leader Success,* states the following about being excellent. This translates to administrative professionals as well:

"To unlock your full potential, one must walk in excellence and be effective in life. The individual who can successfully unlock his/her full potential is able to hit the target, on target. They understand the power of being purposed and assigned to do a task. They never do it alone; unless assigned to do so. They seek strong and wise counsel, and they encourage others to excel in an outstanding manner. No matter the task, they seek ways to improve and excel in extraordinary ways. Excellence does not stop until the task is done well and the solution is effective.

In one of my assignments I noticed there was a man who always wore a rosebud on his lapel. His nickname preceded him. Let's affectionately call him Mr. R. Bud (Mr. Bud never knew that twenty-five years later I would remember this). He was a calm and kind man. He never met a stranger. I would stare at him and the rose on his lapel every time I saw him. He never missed a day wearing the rose bud. He only wore a bud, never a fully opened rose. He always went beyond his peers to get his tasks done well. He was effective, efficient, and excellent (and different) inside and out.

Consider the growth process of a rose. A rose will open up and expose its excellent nature when exposed to water and the proper light. You might be like the rosebud, waiting for the right nurturing and opportunity to reach your full potential. Don't wait; seek out assignments that will help you learn a new skill or to further develop your current skill set. Seek voluntary opportunities such as helping in community efforts to assist future leaders or the elderly. You will find that volunteering will help grow you toward a place of excellence.

There may be others who need a more focused assignment to excel. It is like sharpening a pencil lead–focus on it until it gets sharp and to the point.

Full potential is unlocked through excellent people. They make things happen. They have an understanding about the power of the rose. As long as it is in the light and watered–its glory (its potential) will come forth. To unlock your full potential, seek the right light/instruction/path that will cause you to grow dramatically. Become a learner of excellence. Live by that standard daily. By living a lifestyle of being excellent, others will follow your lead.

It has been said that, "Every person can be a leader. Yet results of surveys show that many men and women greatly underestimate their ability to influence." Whether you are just realizing it or not, you are created to be an excellent leader and an influencer. To make the most of your influence and to assist you in being an excellent leader, study the following principles:

1. *Have the ability to dream–reframe your thinking to realize your full potential. Set an example for excellence for others.*

2. *Know your vision and mission for life.*

3. *Develop a plan and work toward the plan.*

4. *Use your ability to transform the lives of those around you.*

5. *Use your ability to lead with passion and power.*

6. *Know how to leverage your best skills to get things done.*

7. *Strive for excellence in every area of life.*

8. *Be persistent; do what others are not willing to do or cannot do, and do it well.*

9. *Be willing to stand for what you believe and value.*

10. *Change is inevitable; be ready for it."*

Administrative Reflections:

In the space below, list additional thoughts about being excellent in every area of your life. What are your expectations for the future? In what areas are you a different "budding rose"? Who are the people that you trust to share your challenges with? (List 3-5)

10. Let Your Network Work

I have met people who have never met any strangers. On the other hand, it takes a great deal of effort to talk to others. I talked to a gentleman once who said it would sap him to talk to too many excited people during the day.

In either situation, the people all had great relationships with co-workers and others in the workplace. They met new people all the time and kept up with them over the years.

With the myriad of advancements in technology, there are many ways to network and meet new people. At some point in time we all will need to interface with others in life. We must develop new relationships/friendship and teammates to make nearly everything we do work well.

Networking means to be connected or linked with someone. Simply put – to make a connection. I believe many connections are meaningful to you and will enable you to be powerful and impactful in life.

This chapter is brief because I have an exercise for you to compete.

Here it goes:

- On a separate sheet of paper, write down the names of twenty people you know that you met this year at work.
- Write down twenty people you met outside of work on the same sheet.
- One the sheet (or in your book), go to your goals and identify whether any of these connections could generate solutions, help or coach you in reaching your goals. If you are not sure, then for the next few months, notice your connections with your goals in mind. You may have the very solution or help you need in achieving your goal right in front of you.
- List five people who live in different states that you have met recently. What did you learn from them?

- If you needed help finding a friend a job, whom could you call to help you? Make a list.
- If you needed a mentor or coach, who would you call to help you? Make a list.
- If you needed to know about a restaurant across town from where you live, who would you call? Make a list.
- If you need a doctor whom you can trust, who would you call and ask?
- In making your lists, is there any newfound information about your network?
- If you get into trouble and need help with your car (or a ride into work for a week), who could help you with that? Make a list of five people.
- Do you need more people with whom to be connected? Or do you have a big enough net already?

Administrative Reflections:

Close your eyes for a moment. Think about the exceptional relationships that you have had. Think about how they made you feel and what outstanding accomplishments you were able to achieve through those relationships. Smile.

11. Be Honest and Honor

How do you tell someone that they have a piece of lettuce leaf between their teeth or lip-gloss on their teeth? How do you tell someone that there is lint in their hair or that a spider is on their shoulder?

Honesty is best in all cases, but honesty first requires that you to be honest with yourself. As leaders, administrative professionals should be honest and speak with integrity.

The tooth scenario is easy, but there are other circumstances that are not so easy to deal with. In my past, I remember other people telling me to check my teeth, or some would motion with their finger and tell me to "do like this" – while running their finger between their teeth, others would just stare at me until I asked what they were looking at. (LOL!)

Honesty also includes dealing with the difficult conversations and discussions. Honesty includes dealing with the internal or mental instead of the emotional. Honesty is following the process just as it is intended each time. Honesty requires forthrightness and faithfulness in doing things right.

When you do things correctly, it should honor your leader. Honoring your leader requires you to give your very best every time. I know you are tired sometimes and have competing interests, but do the best you can without over stressing yourself. Be honest with yourself, and if you need help, ask for it. If you need more to do – ask for that too.

Honoring your leader is bigger and more than just doing a great job when they are around. True honor suggests how you will act when they are not around.

There was a leader that needed to go away on a long trip. The leader had four workers in his group. One was a great manager and was given many assignments to complete while the boss was gone, the second was given less responsibility, the third even less that the first or the second one. The last employee was only given one task to compete while the boss was away.

The boss came back from his long trip and it was time for a performance review. The first worker had done wonderfully well for the company. He had increased bookings by 50% and had gained more profit for the company. The second worker did equally as well. He had doubled his sales and gained profit for the company. The third had doubled his earnings, bookings, and had created profit and cash for the company. When the last worker was called in for his performance review, he said to the leader, "You went away and I knew you were a hard boss. I did not gain anything for the company I just sat and answered the phones. I was not creative in gaining new business for the company and gained no cash for our business."

The boss was angry. He had left all four workers in charge to do a great job with honesty and integrity. The last worker did not give her best. Needless to say, the boss gave the employee a 'Needs to Improve' rating and the employee did not receive a merit increase that year.

There is still hope! The next year, the employee sought very hard to do better work, increased in knowledge that would benefit the company in unique ways, and made cash for the company. In that same year, what seemed hopeless, turned out to be of great gain to the company. Because of her honest response, even though she had not fully and completely honored the boss – she won, the leader won, and the company gained. All were successful!

Administrative Reflections:

In the space below, make a list of the things you can start doing right away to be honest. What can you do better in your job or community to be more honest and/or honor your leader in a better way?

12. Inspire Others

Inspiration is the ability to encourage others in a way that uplifts them, comforts them or encourages them. When you inspire others, I believe you will be inspired as well. It is part of a principle called sowing and reaping. You are meant to help others and for others to help you. The concept here is very practical and never fails – what you personally invest will be directly proportionate to what you can expect to receive. There is a saying that states: "With the same energy you use, it will be measured back to you." Teamwork makes things work.

As an administrative professional, if you want to inspire others and lead with authority, be willing to invest the time into becoming the professional that you expect to become. Do not sit around waiting for things to happen. Go out and make things happen around you – become a great motivator of others and an encourager. Also, encourage yourself along the way.

In order to inspire others, there are some essential ingredients needed:

1. Be confident and know your strengths. Encourage others to find their strengths. Help them to identify where they make the best contribution. Be creative – keep searching until you find it.
2. Strive for excellence. Remember that the people on your team will not rise to a higher standard of excellence than that which they observe first in you.
3. Set the example in all you do. Others will follow.
4. Encourage others by the way you talk. Encouragers are gifted to find a kind word for others that stirs them, lifts them and even shifts their total attitude or demeanor.

To inspire others and a person of influence in your workplace, school, home, or community, you must first believe from within that you can influence others. I believe you have the ability to do anything you put your mind to. Inspire with the right motive – to encourage or uplift others. I believe there are laws that govern us when we seek to do things the wrong way. The end result is that our wrong efforts will eventually cause us to end up going nowhere.

Inspire others - knowing you encouraged another person can be truly rewarding.

Try it! You will be amazed at the results. I know it works…I tried it and although I may not have received a "thank you" every time, I choose to feel rewarded on the inside. I do not take my blessings for granted. I continue to plant seeds by coaching and leading and inspiring others to be greater. I am very grateful for the opportunity–it works!! Now, go and plant by inspiring others, mentoring, coaching or helping someone by sowing a seed of greatness and reaping an outstanding return!

Administrative Reflections:

In the space below, make a list of one person you can encourage today. What can you do better in your job or community to be an administrative professional that inspires others?

Conclusion

You are a champion. You have so much greatness inside of you waiting to come out of your being. If you believe, then you have what you say and believe. Be faithful to being the best you can be. This mini-book will serve as a great foundation or platform to take you to higher heights.

I am so excited about your success. Do not get discouraged along the way. Destiny is just around the corner, down the block, or a step away. We must learn to see life through a different set of lenses. How exciting!

By now, you should be well on the way to being a better administrative professional. As I stated in the introduction, you are a person of great influence, significance and you have great potential. This book was developed to give you principles to help you soar and do great things; whether you want to be a better professional, parent, student or employee. It is also to help you navigate through the ridges to a place of confidence and contentment.

I believe that you already have exactly what you need inside of you to be the best you. We just need a little boost, tweaking, or education for our confidence to be built to see the greatness within. Sometimes we just need a few adjustments and some enlightenment to see it.

As an administrative professional – as you use this book, it is my belief that you will experience remarkable improvement in their situation, relationships and their performance at many levels. Those who act on what they learn will develop the skills needed to reach the peak states in the organizations they serve.

I believe we all have been granted the ability to accomplish great things. Greatness has many facets and levels. Greatness carries power; and the power to carry out our tasks can be done well with the right desire.

12 Power Principles for Office (Administrative) Professionals, will serve to equip you with tools that will provide valuable insights into how to support your organization or family with greatness. Administrative professionals who use the principles in this book will have an opportunity to transform themselves and others around them on a routine basis. Admins who have a great attitude, create the right atmosphere, use their unlimited potential, use their roadmap, know when to innovate, influence others, think critically, make a difference in excellence, and are honest champions.

We trust that by implementing the principles in this book and creating more of your own, you will begin to see remarkable improvement in your relationships and in your performance at all levels, and you will allow them to make things happen around you.

This book was meant to stir up your thinking and cause you to be more creative, enhance your knowledge, and develop a style that will impact others around you with power. Continue to keep an open mind so that you will be able to see how walking in the authority of a leader will continue to affect you. This will enable you to learn new skills to transform your thinking and touch those whose lives you influence.

Thank you for reading my book. Enjoy your journey as you continue to live powerfully in life!!

I look forward to seeing you in the next leadership mini-book!!

Bibliography

Dr. Amanda Goodson. *Authority of a Leader.* Tucson, AZ, 2012.

Dr. Amanda Goodson. *Powerful People Lead.* Tucson, AZ, 2012.

Dr. Amanda Goodson. *Seed Planting Harvest Expecting Workbook.* Tucson, AZ, 2012.

Frederick Cross, Amanda Goodson and Odetta Scott. *Unlock Your Full Potential.* Tucson, AZ, 2013

Regina Grant, Dena Yell. *Achieving Excellence as an Executive/Management Support Assistant Presentation.* 1998.

Wikipedia. Definition: Achievement.

Businessdictionary.com. Definition: Achievement oriented leadership.

About the Author:

Dr. Amanda H. Goodson

Amanda is an author, educator, facilitator, inspirational speaker and coach for corporations, agencies and non-profit organizations. Amanda inspires others and connects with her audiences by sharing real-life experiences using enthusiastic, energizing, and interactive methods. Amanda has a Bachelor's of Science in Electrical Engineering, a Master's of Science in Management, and a Doctorate degree.

To contact Dr. Amanda Goodson

Email:
ntsminsitries@aol.com

Or visit:
www.AmandaGoodson.com

For a complete listing of CDs, DVDs, and books by Dr. Amanda Goodson, or to participate in a ministry conference, book a conference, speaking event or training, please email or visit the following web site:

NTSMinistries@aol.com
or visit
amandagoodson.com

Leadership books by Dr. Amanda Goodson

Leadership Minibooks™
The Authority of a Leader
Character of a Leader
Unlock Your Full Potential
12 Power Principles for Administrative
Professionals

www.ingramcontent.com/pod-product-compliance
Lightning Source LLC
Chambersburg PA
CBHW032015190326
41520CB00007B/483